TheFire That Did Not Burn Me

NISHA VISHWAKARMA

(For everything that tried to destroy you – and couldn't.)

e people write books.
Ɔthers survive them.
This is both."

BlueRoseONE.com
Stories Matter
NewDelhi • London

BLUEROSE PUBLISHERS
India | U.K.

For permissions requests or inquiries regarding this publication, please contact:

BLUEROSE PUBLISHERS
www.BlueRoseONE.com
info@bluerosepublishers.com
+91 8882 898 898
+4407342408967

ISBN: 978-93-7310-897-1

Cover Design: Aman Sharma
Typesetting: Pooja Sharma

First Edition: September 2025

Dedication

To the one who was never rescued –
but kept rising anyway.

To the heart that kept beating
while it was breaking.

To the soul that kept believing
while it was doubting.

To the person who carried too much
and asked for too little.

This is for the nights you survived in silence.
For the words you swallowed.
For the tears no one saw.

For the hope that flickered but never fully went out.

For the times no one showed you the way forward,
but life kept teaching you –
sometimes harshly –
what should never be done.

This book is a love letter
to that quiet, enduring version of you –

the one who held on with both hands
when everything in you wanted to let go.

You never needed anyone to save you.
You were always saving yourself.

And if no one has ever said this before...

I see you.
I honour you.
This was always meant for you.

Special Thanks

To my **parents** –

For believing in me, even in the moments I couldn't recognize myself.

For being the kind of love that doesn't ask for anything in return – only that I rise.

You showed me what it means to be held by something real, steady, and safe.

You were my first home, and still are.

To my **siblings** –

your faith in me has been louder than my fears.

You reminded me, without ever saying much, that I am never walking alone.

In your belief, I found strength. In your love, I found the courage to keep becoming.

To **every soul who's crossed my path** –

some of you became blessings,

some became lessons,

and a few became stories I'll never retell – but will always carry.

You've all played a part in my becoming –

whether through love, hurt, kindness, silence, betrayal, or support.

Thank you... for being chapters in my journey.

And to my **Almighty – Mahadev** –

the One who held me when the world turned its back.

When I was sinking in silence, when the ocean of life felt endless and cold,

when I gasped for air and it burned like fire –

You stayed.

You held my soul when my body had nothing left.

You stayed when I broke,

and You stayed when I bloomed.

For every unseen miracle,

for every breath You placed in me when I was ready to give up –

Har Har Mahadev.

My gratitude will always belong to You.

Prologue

I didn't write this book to teach you how to fix your life.

I wrote it because sometimes, we aren't meant to be fixed –

we're meant to be seen,

held in the truth of everything we carry but never speak.

There are wounds we learned to live with long before we understood them.

Childhood scars we buried so deep,

they became part of who we thought we had to be.

We learned how to smile when we wanted to scream,

how to forgive before we even understood the weight of betrayal,

how to survive in silence

just to make sure we didn't make things harder for others.

We held in the anger,

remembered every wrong,

carried the bitterness that flared up over the smallest inconveniences –

not because we wanted to,

but because no one ever taught us how to let it go.

We gave –

every inch of our potential,

every soft part of our hearts,

every silent hope –

only to realize sometimes,

No amount of giving is enough to earn what you deserve.

We spent years fixing things we didn't break.

Holding together pieces of people, relationships, and situations

that were supposed to hold us –

but never did.

And somewhere in between,

we started making do with the bare minimum.

We convinced ourselves that surviving was enough,

that asking for more was too much,

that keeping the peace mattered more than keeping ourselves whole.

I wrote this for that part of you.

The part that's exhausted but keeps showing up.

The part that forgives but never forgets.

The part that keeps holding everything together

– even when no one's holding you.

This is not a book of answers.

It's a soft place to land.

A quiet reminder that you're not weak for carrying it all.

That your softness is not your fault.

That your survival is a story worth honouring.

The fire didn't burn you.

It shaped you.

And though you're tired, though you've bent beneath the weight of it all...

You are still here.

You don't need anyone's permission to be proud of how far you've come.

You don't need to explain why it was hard.

You are here – and that, in itself, is everything.

This book is my way of standing quietly beside you,

To remind you –

you were never meant to shrink for the comfort of others,

never meant to carry it all alone,

never meant to apologize for surviving the way you did.

You are allowed to take up space.

You are allowed to begin again –

without permission,

without guilt,

without fear.

You are not here to be small.

You are here to rise – fully, fiercely, and without apology

Let this be the start of everything you thought you weren't allowed to become.

Content

Part I –
The Unraveling *(Pain, Loss, Identity)*

Chapter 1
The Weight We Don't Speak Of

"There are things we carry that we've never put into words – because we were never given the space, the safety, or the language to say them."

There's a kind of weight that doesn't live in your arms or back –

but in your **chest,**

in your **breath,**

in the **space between your thoughts.**

It's the weight of being strong for too long.
Of answering "I'm fine" when you're not.

Of carrying a thousand unspoken moments –
grief, regret, confusion, heartbreak, and hope –
that never found their way into words.

This weight isn't loud.
It doesn't scream for attention.
It just sits there – quietly –
invisible to everyone but you.

You carry it through meetings,

through relationships, through ordinary mornings.

You laugh.

You work.

You help others.

And still – it sits inside you, like a truth you've been too afraid to tell.

Where It Comes From?

It starts early –

long before we know how much it will stay with us.

Sometimes, it's a parent who loved us only when we did what they wanted.

Sometimes, it's a friend who left without a reason.

Sometimes, it's a heartbreak that didn't break us in one moment –

but slowly broke us, little by little.

It's when you needed someone

but didn't ask for help

because deep down,

you already knew they wouldn't come.

It's the moment you realized

no one really saw

how much you were trying to hold everything together.

So, you stayed quiet.

You held it all inside.

You called it "being strong" –
not because you wanted to be,
but because no one ever told you
it was okay to fall apart.
But that wasn't the only weight you carried.
You started expecting too much from yourself.
You tried to be everything for the people you loved.
You gave your time, your care, your love –
even when you had nothing left.
You gave others the love you never got.
You helped the younger ones
the way no one helped you.
You tried to fix things,
to make everyone happy,
to hold everyone together –
even when you were falling apart yourself.
And sometimes...
you just wished for a simple life.
A peaceful life.
The kind of life where you didn't have to fight so hard every single day.
But that's not how life went.
Instead, you stood there,
Watching the people you loved get hurt,
watching them suffer,
and no matter how hard you tried –

you couldn't save them.

You saw everything.

You felt everything.

But all you could do... was watch.

And that hurt more than anyone ever knew.

So you carried that pain too.

Because that's what you've always done.

It's that strange ache in your chest when the world goes quiet, and you finally have time to feel.

And so... you don't.

You distract yourself.

You bury it.

You become "strong."

Not because you never wanted to fall apart –

but because no one ever said it was okay to.

"There's a version of you the world never saw – the one who broke silently. That version deserves to be seen, held, and healed."

What It Does?

Unspoken weight doesn't vanish.

It becomes overthinking.

It becomes anxiety.

It becomes the urge to be perfect, or the fear of taking up space.

It becomes your fear of being "too much."

Your guilt for resting.

Your silence when you should've spoken.
It becomes the apology that lives in your throat
even when you've done nothing wrong.

And Still, You Carried It

Through everything.
You got up.
You worked.
You listened.
You smiled.
You gave love when you didn't receive it.
You held others when you needed to be held.
You did everything right – and still felt heavy.
And that's not your fault.
You were never meant to carry it alone.

What I Wish I Knew Sooner

"The weight we don't speak of becomes the wound we live with.
But the moment we name it – we begin to lift it."

We spend years holding pain we never speak of,
blaming ourselves for the love we didn't get,
and carrying the weight of people and problems
that were never ours to fix.
We try to be everything for everyone –
a helper, a protector, a healer –
and somewhere along the way,
we forget to be kind to ourselves.
But strength doesn't mean
Carrying the world on your shoulders.
And love doesn't mean
Losing yourself while trying to save others.
It's okay to lay down the weight
You've been holding for too long.
It's okay to stop expecting more
From yourself than you'd ever expect from anyone else.
It's okay to let people fight their own battles.
You are allowed to speak your truth.
You are allowed to ask for help.
You are allowed to choose peace over proving your worth.

Letting go is not weakness.

It's the first step toward freedom.

And sometimes, the strongest thing you'll ever do

is finally choose yourself.

You're not wrong for being tired.

You're not weak for needing softness.

You're not alone in this quiet ache.

Speak it.

Write it.

Let it come up – so it can, finally, *leave.*

An Afterword in Poetry

"The Things I Never Said"

There are words
that never made it past my lips—
not because I didn't feel them,
but because I didn't think anyone
would stay long enough to listen.
There are nights I held myself
like a fragile secret,
too afraid to break,
too tired not to.
I have smiled
with a storm in my chest,
answered "I'm okay"
while my soul whispered,
"Help me."
I've learned how to walk
with invisible wounds,
how to laugh with a heart
half missing.
I carried pain like a second skin,
quietly, gracefully,
because no one ever taught me
how to set it down.
But I am unlearning silence now.

I am giving shape to the shadows,
breath to the buried,
and space to the ache.
Not all healing is loud.
Sometimes it's just the courage
to whisper your truth
into the light
and let it live there
without shame.

Chapter 2
The Ache of Almost

"Not all heartbreaks are loud. Some come quietly and live forever."

There are some heartbreaks we don't talk about –

the kind that never fully happened,

but somehow still hurt.

The kind that lives in the silent spaces of "what could have been."

As children, it's missing the school trip you waited for all year,

because you fell sick the night before.

It's the prize you almost won but lost at the last second,

the birthday party you dreamed of but never got,

It's missing out on your dream college by a single mark.

It's giving your best in an exam,

an interview,

a competition –

and falling short by a tiny, cruel inch.

It's being almost enough for someone

Who still chose someone else.

It's standing on the edge of your dreams,

watching them slip through your fingers,

and pretending it doesn't break you.
It's the job you almost got,
the business you built from scratch
that almost took off
– until life forced you to let it go.

It's the relationship that almost became everything you wanted...
but didn't.
It's the love that felt right,
but happened at the wrong time.
And no matter how much you tell yourself to move on,
a part of you still wonders what it could have been.
And then there are the sacrifices no one talks about.
The family duties you couldn't turn away from,
the people you watched suffer
while you stood there, helpless.
The moments you almost stood up,
almost fought back,
almost saved someone –
but couldn't.
And the silent guilt that followed you for not doing more,
even when you gave all you could.

The hardest part?

No one claps for the things that *almost* happened.

No one says, "I'm sorry," for the things you nearly had.

But you remember.

You feel it –

in the quiet moments,

in the places you don't talk about.

The truth is...

the ache of almost is real.

It's not weaker than heartbreak.

It's not smaller than a loss.

It's just quieter.

But it doesn't mean you're weak for feeling it.

It means you cared.

It means you tried.

It means you had a heart open enough to hope –

and that is never something to be ashamed of.

Not everything you lose makes a loud sound.

Some losses are soft, silent, and invisible –

but they shape you just the same.

And even if the world never saw your "almost"

They helped you grow.

They made you softer.

They made you stronger.

They taught you how to stand up after falling apart quietly.

You may not have gotten everything you wanted.
But in trying, in hoping, in almost becoming –
you became something even more powerful.
And maybe... that was the point all along.

The Lessons I Learned From Almost

I learned that "almost" can hurt just as much as a goodbye.
That sometimes, it's not the endings that break you –
it's the things that never really began.
I learned that giving your heart, even without a guarantee,
is a kind of courage most people don't speak about.
I learned that trying – even when it leads to nothing –
is still a form of strength.
Because wanting something, hoping for it,
means you dared to believe in more.
I learned that not everything you chase is meant to be yours,
and sometimes... that's a gift in disguise.
I learned that some people are meant to walk with you
for a little while – not a lifetime.
They come to awaken something inside you,
to teach you something about love, letting go, or yourself.
I learned that "almost" doesn't mean I wasn't enough.
It means it wasn't meant for me.
And that's a truth I had to grow into.
But most of all,
I learned that even unfinished stories
leave behind lessons worth carrying.
And maybe,
not getting what I wanted

helped me become exactly who I was meant to be.

And perhaps the greatest lesson is this:

"You don't need a perfect ending
to grow from an unfinished story."

Chapter 3
The Loneliest Question: Who Am I Now?

"There comes a moment after the 'almost' becomes 'never' –

when you're left standing in the ruins of what could have been...

asking yourself the hardest question of all:

Who am I now?"

No one warns you about the strange kind of emptiness

that follows after you survive the things you thought would break you.

When the person leaves quietly.

When the dream dissolves without explanation.

When the "almost" turns into "never."

And you wake up in a life that looks familiar –

but somehow doesn't feel like your own anymore.

There's a silence after survival.

A stillness that hums beneath the noise of everyday life.

And in that quiet, a question you didn't expect:

"Now what?"

And softer still...

"Who am I now?"

You're not the one curled up on the floor anymore.

Not the one begging to be seen, loved, or saved.

Not the one holding everything together for people

who would've let you fall apart.

You walked away from the burning house.

You stopped the bleeding.

You even started breathing again.

But in the ashes of everything you let go,

you realized –

you're not the same person

who walked into the fire.

When Identity Shifts Quietly

Maybe you were the one who held the family together –

not because you never struggled,

but because falling apart never felt like an option.

The friend who swallowed their own pain

for the sake of keeping peace,

choosing silence over conflict,

because losing people felt heavier than losing yourself.

The person who gave everything in love,

even when nothing came back –

staying when walking away would have been kinder to your heart,

believing that loyalty meant enduring,
even at the cost of your own wellbeing.
Maybe your entire identity became tied
to being something for someone else –
their safe place,
their fixer,
their silent support,
their constant.
And when they left...
or when you finally chose to let go...
you found yourself standing in front of the mirror,
searching for something familiar,
and realizing...
you didn't quite recognize the reflection staring back.
Not because you were broken,
but because somewhere along the way,
you shaped yourself to survive.
A version of you
that lived for approval,
that shrank to stay loved,
that hid feelings to avoid rocking the boat –
and now,
that version no longer fits.
You outgrew the story you were handed.
The role you took on without choice.

The mask you wore so long
it almost felt like your skin.
But the next chapter?
The truest version of you?
It hasn't fully arrived yet.
And this space –
this quiet, uncertain in-between –
between who you were
and who you're still becoming...
can feel unbearably lonely.
Like standing on the edge of a life
you've never really lived.
But maybe...
this is exactly where you meet yourself –
not as who others needed you to be,
but as who you've always been underneath it all.

What No One Tells You about Healing

Healing isn't just about fixing what hurt you.
It's about slowly removing the layers you built
to protect yourself from pain, fear, and disappointment.
Sometimes, you even miss the version of yourself
who knew how to survive in tough times.
Because, in a strange way,
chaos felt familiar.
Pain was something you understood.

And now... peace feels strange.

Freedom feels empty.

You miss the clear roles that pain gave you –

because at least you knew what to expect.

But now, standing here...

without all the old weight,

without the mask you used to wear,

without the old stories you told yourself...

You feel bare.

Exposed.

Unsure.

And you quietly wonder...

Who am I without my pain?

Who am I without the walls I built?

What do I do now that I'm no longer holding everything together for everyone else?

Healing doesn't happen in a single moment.

Sometimes, it means walking through life feeling unsure,

a little messy,

and still figuring it all out –

and that's perfectly okay.

"You don't become someone new overnight. Sometimes, healing means walking through the world uncertain, unpolished, and beautifully undone."

You Are Not Lost – You Are Uncovering

This isn't the end of you.

It's the soft, quiet beginning of returning to who you really are –

the you that's been hiding under fear, expectations, and all the "almosts."

You are not lost.

You are not broken.

You are gently finding your way back

to the real you –

the one who was always enough.

Even if you don't have it all figured out yet...

that's okay.

Becoming isn't something that happens all at once.

It's a slow, steady unfolding.
And with every small step,
with every truth you speak,
with every boundary you protect –
you are coming home
to yourself.

What I Needed to Tell Myself

I needed to remind myself...
That healing is not about erasing the past –
but about loosening its grip on my heart.
That I'm not here to carry every weight in silence,
or hold together what was never mine to fix.
That it's okay to feel lost sometimes,
because feeling lost means I'm no longer stuck in the same old story.
That I don't have to wear strength like armour every day.
I don't have to prove my worth by carrying more than I can bear.
That letting go doesn't make me weak.
It means I'm finally choosing myself.
That it's not wrong to outgrow the roles I once played,
or to step away from people who only loved the version of me
that served their needs.
And most of all...
I needed to remind myself
that I was never really broken.
I was just unfolding –
slowly finding my way back
to the person I was always meant to be.

"You're not who you were – and that's the point.
You outgrew the version of you who only knew how to survive.
Now, you're learning how to live."

Give yourself permission to be a mystery for a while.
To ask questions without rushing for answers.
To rebuild your life from *alignment*, not fear.
You are not lost.
You are not late.
You are not wrong for not knowing who you are just yet.
You are becoming.
And that's not a crisis –
it's the beginning.

And now I want to ask you...

Who are you – beneath everything you were told to be?

Who are you when you're not carrying the weight for everyone else?

When you're not chasing approval?

When you're not hiding behind strength or silence?

Who are you... really?

Chapter 4
The Exhaustion of Being Enough

"There's a kind of tiredness that sleep can't fix...

The exhaustion of always holding together things that were never meant to rest on your shoulders."

We don't talk enough about this –

The quiet exhaustion of constantly trying to be *enough*

For everyone,

Every time,

In every way.

Not because you think you're a saviour...

But because deep down, you know

If you don't do it –

It might all fall apart.

You become the thread that stitches everything together...

And it's ripping you apart, strand by strand.

You Stay... Because You Know They Might Not Make It Without You

You know your family's peace, unity, or survival might crumble if you stop holding it up with your patience, your strength, your sacrifices.

You don't just carry your life –

You carry theirs too.

Their needs.

Their mistakes.

Their second chances.

And you tell yourself,

"If I don't hold them together... who will?"

You Stay... Because Their Future Feels Like Your Responsibility

You see the younger ones – siblings, cousins, children –

and you know their future depends on the decisions made today.

You push yourself harder; stretch yourself thinner,

because you can't bear the thought of them losing chances

you never had.

You carry their hopes like fragile glass

in your already trembling hands.

You Stay... Because You See the Storm Coming Before They Do

You watch people you love walk into mistakes you can already see unfolding.

You try to warn them.

You try to guide them.

You try – again and again – to shield them from the heartache you know is waiting.

But they don't listen.

Or they repeat the cycle.

And all you can do is stand at the edge...

Watching... Helpless.

You Stay... Because you're Afraid to Let Go

What if they fall apart without you?

What if walking away ruins their life?

What if you stop showing up and everything collapses?

You don't want to be the reason for their failure.

So you stay.

Even when it drains you.

Even when it hurts.

Because the fear of losing them...

feels worse than the pain of losing yourself.

The Exhaustion That No One Sees

The exhaustion of being the fixer.

The exhaustion of giving advice that's ignored.

The exhaustion of holding your pain to protect their peace.

The exhaustion of keeping your life in check so others don't fall apart.

And the worst of all...

The exhaustion of knowing

you're doing everything possible –

and it still may never be enough.

What I Learned Through This Exhaustion

I learned that love doesn't mean saving someone from themselves.

I learned that no matter how much I give,some people will only change when *they* decide to.

I learned that carrying their weight won't fix their mistakes,

It will only break me.

I learned that being there for others should never mean abandoning myself.

I learned that I can want the best for people – and still protect my heart and my peace.

And Now... I Want to Gently Ask You

Who have you been holding together –

while quietly falling apart yourself?

Whose future are you carrying on your tired shoulders...
when it was never meant to rest entirely on you?
When was the last time you looked in the mirror and asked –
"Have I been enough for myself?"
Because maybe...
you've poured yourself out for everyone else,
over and over,
for far too long.
And maybe now...
it's time to finally pour some of that love,
that grace,
that patience...
back into yourself.
You are not failing them by stepping back.
You're saving yourself.
And sometimes –
that's not selfish.
That's survival.
That's courage.
That's choosing life for you...
before you lose yourself completely.

What I Need You to Know About This Exhaustion

If you're anything like me, you've probably believed –

for a long time –

that loving people means saving them.

That if you just try hard enough,

if you give enough of yourself,

they'll change.

They'll listen.

They'll finally see what you've been trying to protect them from.

I used to think that too.

But here's what I learned...

Love doesn't mean carrying someone else's life on your back.

It doesn't mean shielding them from every fall

or fixing every mistake before it happens.

Because no matter how much you care...

people will only change when *they* decide to.

And sometimes... they won't.

I've learned this the hard way –

by breaking myself over and over

trying to hold together lives

that were never mine to fix.

I've learned that carrying someone else's weight

doesn't make me stronger.
It only wears me down,
quietly, relentlessly –
until I have nothing left for myself.
I've learned that being there for others
shouldn't mean abandoning myself in the process.
That sacrificing your peace, your joy, your mental health...
isn't what real love asks of you.
You can want the best for people –
and still protect your heart.
You can care deeply –
without drowning quietly.
And maybe the hardest thing I've learned...
is this:

It's not your failure
when someone refuses to change.

It's not your fault
when they choose a harder road –
even when you warned them.

Your love isn't measured
by how much you suffer for someone else.
You don't have to carry the weight of their choices

to prove your loyalty or love.

You are allowed to set that weight down.

And when you do,

you'll realize you were never heartless for letting go –

you were finally honest with yourself.

Before You Go...

A Letter to the One Who's Tired of Holding It All

I know you've been carrying more than anyone sees.

I know how it feels to watch people lean on you,

while you're quietly falling apart inside.

You've been the strong one.

The fixer.

The safe place.

The silent shield.

But I want to tell you something you may have forgotten:

It is not your job to save everyone.

It is not your duty to carry their futures on your back.

It is not your responsibility to fix the consequences of choices you didn't make.

You are allowed to care deeply –

without breaking completely.

You are allowed to love people fiercely –

without losing yourself in the process.

And you are allowed to rest.

To choose yourself.

To step back, not out of selfishness...

but out of love for the person who's been holding it all together –

YOU.

Because you've done enough.

You've been enough.

And now...

It's your turn to be held.

Even if only by your own hands.

"You don't have to become less of yourself to be more for others."

You are not a project. You are a person.

You are allowed to be enough, simply because you exist.

Not because of your achievements.

Not because of how much you endure.

Not because of how quiet you stay in your pain.

The world may not always validate your worth –

But that doesn't mean it isn't there.

Let this be your soft rebellion:

Stop proving.

Stop performing.

Start **being.**

You are not too much.

You are not not enough.

You are exactly who you were meant to be – growing, hurting, rising, unbecoming, re-becoming.

And you deserve to be loved, not for how much of yourself you sacrifice...

...but for how fully you dare to exist.

Part II
The Shedding *(Letting Go, Boundaries, Growth)*

Chapter 5
The Art of Letting Go

"Letting go is not a moment. It's a process. A quiet choosing of yourself over and over – even when your heart wants to hold on."

We talk so easily about letting go.

We say it to others – "*You just need to let it go.*"

We say it to ourselves – "*It's time. Move on.*"

And sometimes, people even write about it, like it's a checklist...

as if letting go were as simple as snapping your fingers.

But if you've ever been the one trying to actually do it...

you know the truth.

Letting go is not a moment.

It's a long, messy, painful process.

It's a thousand quiet choices you make when the world isn't watching.

It's when memories creep into your mind at 2 AM...

and you sit there, holding back tears,

reminding yourself – again – why you walked away.

It's when you see them happy, moving on...

and you whisper to your heart – "*That's okay. I'm choosing peace.*"

It's when you're lying on your bed,

feeling like life has left you behind,

watching your family and friends try their best to bring you back to life...

but their efforts aren't enough because this battle is yours to fight.

It's when you realize

even after doing everything right,

you still have to let go...

because holding on isn't fixing anything.

From childhood, we're taught so many things:

To love.

To forgive.

To try harder.

To stay strong.

To never give up.

But no one teaches us

that sometimes...

the strongest, bravest thing you can do

is to walk away.

Not because you didn't care.

Not because you didn't try hard enough.

But because holding on started to cost you too much of yourself.

Letting Go Isn't Just About People

We often think letting go means leaving someone.

But sometimes...

it's letting go of dreams that didn't happen.

Letting go of expectations you placed on yourself.

Letting go of the person you thought you'd be by now.

It's saying goodbye to friendships that faded quietly.

To love that once felt safe – until it started hurting more than it healed.

It's letting go of the version of yourself

who thought everything would make sense... if you just tried a little harder.

We hold on because we hope.

But sometimes, hope becomes a silent kind of suffering.

What makes us Keep Holding On?

Sometimes, we don't hold on because we still believe.

We hold on because we're scared of what comes after.

We fear the empty space.

The silence.

The loneliness that might greet us once we finally let go.

What if nothing better comes?

What if this is as good as it gets?

But staying in something that's hurting you

just because you're afraid of what's next...

is how you stay stuck in a story

that was never meant to be your forever.

Your fear of the unknown is real.

But staying in pain – just because it's familiar –

will only leave you living a life that's half-alive.

Letting go doesn't mean you're selfish.

Letting go doesn't mean you're weak.

Letting go doesn't mean you're heartless.

It doesn't mean you gave up too soon.

It means you finally realized that breaking your own heart

for the sake of others

isn't love.

It's slow self-destruction.

You are allowed to choose your peace.

You are allowed to protect your heart.

Letting go is survival.

It's looking at the mirror and saying...

"I deserve peace. I deserve space to breathe. Even if I have to find it alone."

Because if something requires you to break yourself to keep it, it was never meant to be yours.

What Letting Go Really Means?

Letting go isn't about forgetting.

It isn't about pretending it never mattered.

It means giving yourself permission to stop carrying what has been breaking you.

It's choosing peace over pain.

It's choosing your future over a past you can't change.

Letting go means making space –

space for calm,

space for better people,

space for love that doesn't leave you drained,

and space for the life you deserve.

It's like setting down a heavy bag you've been carrying for miles.

Not because it wasn't valuable...

but because it's too heavy to keep holding on your own.

It's realizing you don't have to drag old stories, regrets, or people along -

Just to prove you cared.

Letting go is trusting that your story isn't over yet –

and maybe,

the best parts are still waiting...

once you make room for them.

So if your hands feel tired from holding on...

if your heart feels worn from carrying it all...

maybe it's time to ask yourself –

"What could come into my life...

if I finally made space for it?"

Letting go isn't losing.

It's opening the door to everything you've been too full to receive.

A Gentle Check-In With Yourself

What am I still holding on to?

Why am I holding on to it?

What is it costing me?

How much more of myself will I lose before I finally set it down?

What Letting Go Taught Me

I realized that loving people with all your heart
isn't enough to change them –
because change is something only they can choose.
I learned that sometimes, I held on so tightly
not because I believed things would get better...
but because I was scared of who I'd be without them.
But letting go didn't break me.
It brought me back to myself.
I learned that letting go isn't giving up.
It's giving myself permission to heal...
to rest...
to stop fighting battles I was never meant to fight alone.
And I want you to know...
Holding on doesn't make you strong –
and letting go doesn't make you weak.
Sometimes, the strongest, bravest thing you'll ever do...
is finally choose yourself.

"Letting go isn't the loss of love – it's the return to self."

You don't let go because it meant nothing.

You let go because it once meant everything – and still could not stay.

Letting go does not mean you stop caring.

It means you start caring for **yourself more honestly.**

It is the quiet courage of choosing peace over patterns, truth over attachment, growth over familiarity.

It is the realization that some things are beautiful – and still not meant to last.

That not everything that feels like home is safe to live in forever.

You are not moving on because it didn't matter.

You are moving forward because **you finally matter to yourself.**

Letting go is not a defeat.

It's a declaration: *"I will no longer abandon myself to be held by someone else."*

And in that soft surrender,

you don't lose –

you come back to life.

Chapter 6
The Mess of Healing

"The process of healing hurts more than the pain that made you need it."

Everyone talks about healing like it's a sunrise.

Like it's soft mornings and journaling and tea and peace.

Like it's a glowing transformation – the part of the story where the pain ends and the strength begins.

But healing?

"Healing doesn't feel like healing when you're inside it."

It's chaos before clarity.

It's waking up with a heavy chest and forcing your feet to touch the floor anyway.

It's knowing someone wasn't good for you –

and yet...

still wishing, in some aching corner of your heart,

that they'd walk back through the door.

It's being surrounded by people and still feeling like **you're the only one bleeding.**

It's hearing that one song

—the one that once broke you—

and realizing, out of nowhere,

that it doesn't cut as deep anymore...

And in that strange, quiet moment –

you almost miss the pain.

Because the numbness feels unfamiliar...

and unfamiliar feels scary.

Healing is not a straight line.

It's not a checklist.

And it doesn't come with applause.

We often hear people say, *"Healing takes time."*

But healing isn't just about time –

and it's never a simple path you follow step by step.

You don't need deep healing from a random bad day.

You don't carry wounds from things that brushed past you.

If something requires healing...

it's because it has lived inside you for a long time.

It's because it wasn't just a one-time hurt –

it was a pattern.

A repeated cycle.
A wound that got reopened over and over
until it became part of who you thought you were.
That's why healing feels messy.

Why it feels like progress one day
& like you're drowning the next?

Because you're not just patching up a single crack –
you're untangling years of knots,
breaking patterns you didn't even realize you were stuck in,
letting go of survival habits that once kept you safe,
but now keep you small.

Healing is not a straight line
because real healing means unlearning what pain taught you.
And that unlearning takes courage – and time.

It means falling apart sometimes,
even when you thought you'd already moved on.

It means having days where the old wounds feel fresh again,
and instead of hating yourself for it,
learning to say –
"This is part of it. I'm still healing. And that's okay."

"Healing is ugly, exhausting, and sacred all at once."

Sometimes there are Wounds We Carry from Childhood

Some wounds don't bleed on the outside.

They settle quietly into your heart when you're too young to name them.

Maybe you grew up in a house where love had rules.

Where being "good" meant staying silent when things got loud.

Where you learned it was better to shrink yourself

than risk watching everything – and everyone – fall apart.

Maybe you were the child who held their breath during every argument,

hoping your silence would keep the peace.

Or the teenager who became "the responsible one" –

the one who stayed home when friends went out,

because you couldn't leave your family alone with their own chaos.

Or the kid who tried too hard in school, in sports, at everything...

because praise felt safer than attention,

and achievements were the only way to be seen.

And so, you grew up thinking love had to be earned.

That your worth was measured by how much you could fix,

or how much you could give away without asking anything in return.

You became the helper.

The fixer.

The one who smiled when you wanted to cry.

The one who said, "It's okay, I've got it,"

even when it wasn't –

even when you didn't.

And that role followed you into adulthood.

Into friendships where you gave more than you got.

Into relationships where you forgave too much,

and stayed too long,

because walking away felt like failure.

Into workplaces where you worked twice as hard for half the recognition.

Until one day... you hit a wall.

Not because you were weak –

but because you finally realized...

you've been living your whole life on survival mode.

Always trying to hold everything together –

for everyone else.

And in that moment, you saw it for what it was:

You weren't living.

You were surviving.

And surviving isn't the same as being alive.

There may be someone Who Left Without Saying Goodbye

Maybe you had that friend.

The one you trusted with every piece of your heart.

The late-night talks that stretched till morning.

The secrets you swore you'd never tell anyone else.

The moments when you showed up for them,

even when you were barely holding yourself together.

And then, one day... they left.

No fight.

No explanation.

Just a slow drift into silence,

like you never mattered at all.

For months – maybe even years –

you replayed every word,

every memory,

every text.

"Was it something I said?"

"Did I ask for too much?"

"Was I too much?"

You tore yourself apart looking for the answer

to a question you never even got to ask.

But slowly...

healing showed you something you didn't expect.

Sometimes, people leave –
not because you were wrong...
but because you were real.
Because you grew honest,
and they weren't ready for honesty.

Because you stopped shrinking yourself,
and they only knew how to love you small.
Because you set boundaries,
and they didn't know how to handle your strength.

And sometimes...
they left because it was easier for them to leave
than it was for them to face their own reflection
in the way you loved them.

It hurts – deeply.
But it's not your failure.
It never was.

May be the Love that Left You Empty?
Maybe you loved someone so fiercely,
you started to believe that loving them hard enough
could fill the empty spaces inside both of you.
You gave...

and gave...

and gave –

pouring your heart out like it was endless.

You waited for them to see you.

You hoped they'd meet you halfway.

You believed, deep down,

that if you just loved them right...

they would finally become who you needed them to be.

But they didn't.

They didn't change.

They didn't give back.

They only kept taking –

until you felt like a shadow of yourself.

And the part that hurt the most?

It wasn't just that they didn't love you back.

It was realizing...

you were loving them

in all the ways you wished someone would love you.

You were trying to give them

the kindness, the patience, the care,

that you never received.

Loving them became your silent way of begging the universe

to give you what you never got.

But that's the thing about pouring into the wrong hands –

They'll let you empty yourself completely...

And walk away like it meant nothing.

There can be a thousand reasons for pain –

Maybe you missed a chance you thought would change everything.

Maybe the job, the opportunity ... slipped away.

It doesn't matter how unexpected or unfair it was –

What happened, happened.

We can't change that.

But what we **can** do...

is choose to heal from it.

Because healing isn't about pretending it didn't hurt.

It's about refusing to let that hurt become the story of who you are.

Because when you stop accepting what used to hurt you, the world doesn't always clap for you – sometimes, it gets quieter.

As much as healing is necessary...

healing can also feel deeply isolating.

You may lose people.

You may lose routines that kept you numb.

You may outgrow things that once felt like comfort.

And it will feel like loss, because it is.

But that's how healing works –

it takes away what no longer fits, even if you weren't ready to let it go.

You'll cry in places you once laughed.

You'll feel the sting of absence more than the relief of space.

You'll grieve your old self – even the parts that were just coping.

And yet, slowly, something shifts.

Not with fireworks, but in tiny moments.

You'll laugh – for real – and surprise yourself.

You'll notice you didn't check their profile this week.

You'll sit in silence and feel peace instead of panic.

You'll look in the mirror and finally **recognize the eyes looking back.**

"Healing is not about becoming someone new. It's about remembering who you were before the world taught you to forget."

A Moment from My Own Journey

I remember one night, sitting on the floor of my room –

my leg aching after a fracture that felt like both a wound and a pause I hadn't asked for.

No job.

No results from the endless exams I had poured my heart into.

Each failure felt heavier than the last.

Not just because of what I lost –

but because I started losing little pieces of myself with every rejection.

By then, I had distanced myself from almost every friend.

Not out of anger,

but because I couldn't fake the smile anymore.

I was the eldest child in my family –

three younger siblings watching me,

waiting for me to set the example,

while I was crumbling under the weight of dreams

that felt impossible to reach.

And then there were my own expectations –

my silent list of things I thought I *should* have been by now.

Successful. Settled. Strong.

But instead... I was sitting in a silent room,

waiting on a message I knew would never come.

It wasn't even about the person anymore.

It was about how much I had given to people

who never gave anything back.

It hurt –

not because I needed them,

but because I hated that I still cared.

That I still waited.

That after everything...

I still hadn't learned how to stop hoping.

And in that quiet, almost unbearable moment,

I asked myself, out loud:

"Why am I still waiting on someone who never showed up for me?"

That question didn't fix everything.

But it cracked something open in me.

For the first time, I realized...

I was not just waiting on people.

I was waiting on life.

Waiting on someone or something to come save me.

And maybe...

maybe I needed to stop waiting.

The change didn't happen overnight.

There were still days when I lay in bed staring at the ceiling.

Still nights when I felt like I was drowning in my own thoughts.

Still moments when I wanted to give up.

But slowly – painfully slowly – I started choosing myself.

I got up.

I studied again.

I healed my leg.

I worked on the small things that felt too silly to matter – until they started mattering.

I laughed at stupid jokes with my siblings.

I made tea for my parents without being asked.

I started rebuilding friendships with people who saw me for more than my failures.

I gave myself permission to start small...

and in those small moments, I started becoming myself again.

One morning, I realized –

I was not waiting for that message anymore.

The ache had not disappeared.

But I had stopped letting it define me.

I looked in the mirror and thought,

"You're still here. You're still standing. And that's enough."

It was not a fairy tale ending.

But it was real.

I didn't get everything I dreamed of right away.

But I found something better –

a peace that didn't depend on anyone else.

A quiet knowing that I was going to be okay –

because I wasn't giving up on myself anymore.

And maybe...

that's the happiest ending I could have ever asked for.

The Butter

"Healing doesn't always look like growth – sometimes, it looks like stillness, silence, or even breaking. But every moment you choose to feel, you're choosing to live."

It's not about feeling better every day.

It's about showing up for yourself on the days you feel nothing at all.

It's not about fixing what broke.

It's about learning to live with the cracks – and letting light come through them.

Healing is not soft music, scented candles, or sunlight streaming in.

It's trembling hands reaching for water when your soul feels dry.

It's crying without knowing why.

It's telling yourself, *"I'll try again tomorrow,"* even when today felt like drowning.

It's forgiving yourself for the person you had to become to survive.

It's honoring the version of you that kept going when everything begged you to stop.

Some wounds will always whisper.

But healing is the quiet decision to no longer let them define your story.

Because healing isn't a finish line.

It's a quiet, daily rebellion.

A sacred act of defiance against the weight of what tried to break you.

And every time you choose to keep breathing through the storm —

you are already becoming whole.

Chapter 7
Becoming Your Own Home

We spend most of our lives searching for a place to land –

A space where we can breathe without being told we're too loud,

Love without shrinking ourselves,

Exist without explanation.

As children, we look for that safety in our parents' approval.

As teenagers, in peer groups that feels more like tests than connections.

And as adults, we often pour our hearts into friendships, relationships, and careers...

hoping someone, somewhere, will finally say,

"You – just as you are – are enough."

But sometimes the places we call "home" make us feel lonelier than silence ever did.

We all want to belong.

It's one of the most natural human desires –

to feel seen, heard, and accepted

for simply being who we are.

But somewhere along the way,

we begin to confuse *belonging* with *performing*.

We start to believe that to be loved, we must first be *pleasing.*

That to be accepted, we must first *adjust.*

That to stay close to people, we must make ourselves *smaller.*

We call it **connection,**

but deep down, it feels more like being *tolerated* – not embraced.

Proximity is not the same as connection.

Just because someone sits beside you

doesn't mean they see you.

Just because someone shares your memories

doesn't mean they hold your heart.

We call it **community,**

but it's often built on convenience, not care –

a place where you're welcome only when you follow the unspoken rules.

We call it **love,**

but it disappears the moment we stop hiding the parts of us

that are "too much," "too loud," or "too real."

The Cost of Being Easy to Love

Many of us go through life as quiet shape-shifters.

Not because we're deceitful,
but because we've learned – often from a young age –
that being *ourselves* isn't always safe, accepted, or appreciated.
So we adjust.

We wear masks labelled **"easy-going"**
so no one calls us "too emotional."

We take on the title **"helpful"**
so we're always useful – even when we're exhausted.

We pretend to be **"low-maintenance"**
so we never seem like a burden, even when we're breaking.

We silence our opinions in conversations
so we won't be called difficult.

We push our needs aside
so we can hold space for everyone else's.

We laugh at jokes that hurt us,
nod in rooms where our voices go unheard,
and stay in roles, friendships, and relationships
that ask us to keep proving our worth.

We learn how to blend in,
how to smooth our edges,
how to become versions of ourselves
that are easier to love – or at least, easier to tolerate.

And at first, it seems to work.
People like us.
We're invited, included, even praised.
But beneath the surface, a quiet ache begins to grow.
Because something heart breaking happens over time:
We begin to forget who we were
before we became who the world asked us to be.

The lines between *who we are*
and *who we perform to be* start to blur.

Psychologists call this **self-abandonment** –
when we repeatedly choose external comfort over internal truth.

Philosophers might call it **losing the Self** –
a disconnection from our soul's own voice.
But no matter what language you use,
the feeling is the same:
It's like standing in the middle of your own life

and not recognizing the person living it.

You look around and see all the roles you've filled:

The good daughter.

The strong friend.

The calm one.

The dependable one.

The one who never asks for too much.

But where are *you* in all of that?

Where is the person who had dreams before they were edited for practicality?

Where is the one who used to speak freely before learning to filter every word?

Where is the version of you that was once vibrant, wild, unsure – but **real**?

That's the wound so many of us carry quietly:

The ache of not feeling at home in our own lives –

not because we're in the wrong place,

but because we've gone missing inside the right one.

But the story doesn't end there.

The beautiful – and painful – truth is:

You can return to yourself.

It starts slowly.

With small acts of honesty.

With saying "no" when you mean it.

With asking, "What do *I* want?" before offering yourself to everyone else.

With choosing truth over likeability.

And with giving yourself permission to take up space –

without explanation.

Coming home to yourself isn't always comfortable.

You might disappoint people who loved your mask more than your face.

You might feel lonely for a while.

You might even grieve the years you spent away from yourself.

But in time, you'll feel something new – and deeply familiar:

A quiet belonging

that doesn't depend on performance.

A peace that doesn't shrink for approval.

A home you carry inside you, wherever you go.

And this time, it will be real.

"The soul always knows what to do to heal itself. The challenge is to silence the mind."

– Caroline Myss

From Seeking Approval to Returning to Yourself

There comes a moment in life – not always loud, not always dramatic –

but quiet and still, like a whisper in the middle of noise.

A moment when **external validation starts to lose its shine.**

When the compliments that once felt like oxygen
begin to sound hollow.
When the likes on a photo, the praise from a boss,
the reply from someone who once left you unseen –
no longer satisfy the ache inside your chest.
You start to notice it -
That ache isn't for attention.
It's not even for approval.
It's for something far more deeply personal.
It's for truth. For peace. For home.

Because for too long, you've been performing.
Smiling when you wanted to cry.
Saying "I'm fine" when you were breaking.
Chasing applause from people
who only ever saw the polished version of you –
not the full, messy, magical human underneath.
You told yourself if you could just earn their love...
you would finally be okay.
So you shaped yourself into who they wanted.
You softened your voice, swallowed your needs,
worked harder, smiled brighter, stayed quieter –
all in the name of being "enough."
But then, one day –
maybe after a long week, a lonely evening, a deep breath in a quiet room –

you **stop running.**

You sit still.

And you ask, perhaps for the first time in your life:

"What do I need –

not to be loved by them,

but to love being me?"

The question lands like a truth you've always known.

And slowly, gently, the answers begin to rise:

You need **space** – not for performance, but for presence.

You need **rest** – from proving, from pleasing, from perfecting.

You need **boundaries** – not to keep others out,

but to finally let yourself in.

You realize you've been building your worth

on the opinions of people who don't even know your soul.

And now?

Now, you're ready to come home to yourself.

Not the version that's polished and approved.

Not the version that always says yes.

But the version that's **real** –

soft, fierce, tired, healing, whole.

You start choosing silence over noise.

Honesty over performance.

Peace over popularity.

And little by little,

you stop looking for love outside of you

and start building it within you.

This is not the end of your journey –

but it is the beginning of your return.

A return to the *you* that was never too much,

never not enough,

just temporarily hidden beneath layers of "should."

You don't need to earn your worth.

You only need to remember it.

And when you do,

you'll stop waiting to be chosen

and start choosing **yourself.**

Again and again – until it no longer feels like rebellion,

but like coming home.

And slowly, beautifully, you learn that being alone isn't the same as being lonely.

It's peace.

It's truth.

It's belonging.

True belonging has nothing to do with how well you blend in.

It has everything to do with how deeply you stay rooted in who you are.

You were not born to be everyone's cup of comfort.

You were not made to be digestible.

You were made to be **true.**

And truth doesn't need permission to exist.

So let the rooms that can't hold your light feel too dim.

Let the people who can't hear your silence drift into their own noise.

Let the roles that keep you invisible collapse.

Because you deserve more than a seat at a table that doesn't see your soul.

You deserve to build your own – where every version of you is welcomed.

"Stop knocking on doors that close every time you show up fully. The door you're looking for is the one within."

The Lesson:

"You won't find home in people who ask you to leave parts of yourself at the door. You become home the moment you stop seeking permission to exist."

True belonging begins not when others accept you –

but when you refuse to abandon yourself just to be accepted.

You don't need to fit in.

You need to stand still in your own truth and say,

"This is who I am. Unpolished. Unapologetic. Unfolding."

The people meant for you won't flinch at your depth.

The spaces made for you won't shrink your voice.

And the life aligned with your soul won't ask you to become someone else to earn it.

So stop knocking on closed doors.

Stop begging for space in places that leave you empty.

Instead – become the space.

The refuge.

The sanctuary.

Become your own home.

And when you do,

you won't just belong somewhere –

you'll belong **everywhere you dare to be fully yourself.**

Repeat these softly – or fiercely – as often as you need. Let them remind you of the truth you already carry within.

I AM ENOUGH

I do not need to become smaller to be loved.

I am already enough – even in my chaos, even in my quiet.

I BELONG TO MYSELF

I no longer seek homes in places that ask me to abandon who I am.

I am the home I've been searching for.

I RELEASE THE NEED TO FIT IN

I let go of shrinking to be accepted.

I now choose to expand in my truth – even if it means standing alone.

I TRUST MY VOICE

My voice matters – even when it shakes.

I give myself permission to speak, to say no, to ask for more.

I FORGIVE MY PAST

The old versions of me were only trying to survive.

I honour them, and now choose to thrive.

I AM SAFE WITHIN ME

Even when the world feels uncertain,

I carry peace inside me.

I am my own shelter, my own soft place to land.

I CHOOSE ME

Today, I choose to return to myself.

To love myself the way I've always longed to be loved.

Chapter 8
When Growth Feels Like Loss

There was once a butterfly who looked back longingly at her cocoon.

She missed the quiet. The stillness. The familiarity.

Now, with wings wide open, she was expected to fly.

But some days, she only wanted to curl back into the warmth of what used to hold her.

But she couldn't.

The cocoon was too small now.

Too tight. Too dark. Too limiting.

And so she learned –

missing something doesn't mean you belong there.

It just means it mattered once.

And it helped you become who you are today.

We grow.

Day by day, experience by experience, mistake by mistake.

We learn.

Sometimes through books.

Sometimes through heartbreak.

Sometimes through the mistakes of others.

Sometimes through those quiet moments when the world goes still and we realize – *we are no longer the same.*

And that realization can hurt.

The Invisible Price of Maturity

When you grow, the world doesn't change – *you* do.

You begin to notice things.

You hear the tone behind the words.

You feel when something is off – even if nothing is said aloud.

You see the difference between words and actions,

between intention and impact,

between familiarity and true connection.

You begin to read between the lines – not just in others, but in yourself.

You ask:

Why did I react that way?

Why am I still holding on to that?

Is this love – or is this a pattern I'm afraid to break?

That awareness is both a gift and a burden.

Because once you see, you cannot unsee.

And once you understand, you cannot pretend you don't.

You begin to understand what must end –

Not out of resentment,

but out of reverence for your own growth.

You no longer chase energy that leaves you depleted.

You no longer sacrifice your boundaries to keep the peace.

You no longer sit at tables where you have to shrink yourself to be loved.

But the moment you start acting on this clarity – the world resists.

People notice.

They feel the shift – even if you say nothing.

They call it "distance."

They call it "coldness."

They call it *change.*

"You've changed."

Yes.

Because I had to.

Because staying the same began to feel like self-abandonment.

Because pretending to be okay with things I had outgrown started to feel like dishonesty – to them, and to myself.

But this is the part no one prepares you for:

Growth doesn't just change you – it changes your relationships.

Because growth pulls on the threads that connect us.

It tests which ones are elastic – and which were always conditional.

Some relationships stretch with you,

adapting to your evolution,

even if clumsily.

Others snap – too rigid to bend, too rooted in who you used to be.

And when those threads break,

it doesn't always feel like freedom.

Sometimes it feels like loss.

A loss you didn't choose, but had to accept.

You miss the comfort of who you used to be,

even if that version of you was hurting.

You miss the simplicity of not knowing better –

even if it came with chaos.

You miss the people you once fit with –

even if that fit required you to dim your light.

That is the invisible price of maturity:

Losing without a fight.

Leaving without anger.

Letting go without making someone the villain.

Not because they were wrong – but because you are no longer the same.

And pretending otherwise would be the real betrayal.

Understanding without Blame

You don't want to hurt anyone.

You don't want to leave scorched bridges behind you.

You don't want your silence to feel like punishment.

You simply want space to breathe, to be, to become.

You don't want to walk away in bitterness or burn what once felt sacred.

You just want to **end things gently** –

with grace in your step and gratitude in your heart.

To look them in the eyes – perhaps for the last time –

and whisper softly:

"You were good for who I was. But I'm no longer that version of me."

"I don't blame you. I don't resent you. I just can't keep pretending I belong where I've outgrown."

That's not cruelty.

That's clarity.

That's compassion – for yourself *and* for them.

But the world often doesn't see it that way.

People don't always understand when love shifts, when loyalty evolves, when presence turns into absence – not from hate, but from healing.

But here's what growth teaches you:

Not everyone will understand your choices – and that's okay.

Because your growth isn't a group decision.

Your healing isn't up for debate.

Your peace doesn't need approval.

You will disappoint people on this path.

You will be misunderstood.

You may be talked about in rooms where your heart is misquoted.

But here's the thing:

Growth isn't about being understood.

It's about being true.

True to the lessons you've earned.

True to the voice inside you that once begged you to stop shrinking.

True to the life you're building – one aligned decision at a time.

You're not walking away in anger.

You're walking away in love – for who you're becoming.

"You're not leaving people behind. You're just not staying behind with them."

Age Is Not Just a Number

People often say, "*Age is just a number.*"

But it's more than that.

Age is the number of times your heart has broken – and healed.

The number of nights you couldn't sleep because your mind was full of questions.

The books you've read that made you see the world differently.

The people you've met – some who helped you grow, and some who hurt you.

The moments when you kept going, even when all you wanted was to give up.

Age means experience.

It's the quiet wisdom that builds up inside you over time.

As you grow older, things become clearer.

You stop chasing people who don't treat you right.

You stop finding beauty in pain.

You choose peace instead of drama.

You prefer calm over noise.

You start to understand that not every relationship is meant to last forever.

Some people are part of your story, but not your whole journey.

And that's okay.

With age, you learn to respect yourself more.

You know your limits.

You stop explaining yourself to everyone.

You begin to love your own company.

Because in the end, age is not just about how many years you've lived –

It's about how deeply you've felt, how much you've learned, and how far you've come.

"Not everyone is meant to walk with you into who you're becoming."

The Takeaway

"Growth isn't a betrayal – it's a becoming. And becoming yourself fully will always cost you what kept you small."

You don't owe anyone your stagnation.

You don't owe your younger self the safety of staying unchanged.

You are allowed to evolve – even if others preferred the quieter, easier, more agreeable version of you.

And yes, that will come with lonely seasons.

But loneliness is not proof you're doing something wrong.

Its proof you're no longer hiding in the wrong places.

Your soul is shedding the weight of pretending.

Your heart is learning how to beat freely – not perform.

So if you find yourself walking alone right now,

know this:

You're not losing everything.

You're making space.

And the ones who are meant for the next part of your story –

will meet you on the other side of your becoming.

Part III

The Becoming *(Wholeness, Strength, Peace)*

Chapter 9
The Soft Power of Saying No

"You do not need to set yourself on fire to keep others warm.
Let the warmth you offer come from the peace you've kept within."

You say yes to favors you don't have time for.
Yes to conversations that drain you.
Yes to relationships that ask you to prove your worth over and over again.
You say yes when your body is begging for rest.
When your heart is quietly whispering "*please, not this again.*"

And still – you smile.
And still – you say yes.

Because guilt is louder than your exhaustion.
Because you've been told that "no" is unkind.
Because somewhere along the way, you started believing
that love must be earned through sacrifice.

We often think saying **"no"** means we're being rude or pushing people away.
As if "no" means we don't care.

As if it builds walls between us and others.

But that's not always true.

"No" is not always about other people.

Many times, it's about *you* – your peace, your space, your limits.

Saying no is not a bad thing.

It's a way of protecting yourself.

It's how you take care of your energy, your time, and your feelings.

It's not selfish.

It's honest.

You don't say no because you don't care –

You say no because you've *started to care.*

About your mental health.

About your boundaries.

About what truly feels right for you.

Sometimes, "no" simply means:

"I don't have space for this right now."

"I need rest."

"I want to focus on myself."

And that's okay.

You're not rejecting others –

You're finally accepting yourself.

Saying no doesn't make you a bad person.

It just means you're learning to listen to your needs –

and that's something to be proud of.

"You are not unkind for choosing yourself. You are just no longer available to be emptied."

The Philosophy of Enough –

In a world that glorifies "yes" – more hours, more responsibilities, more engagement –

saying no is almost an act of rebellion.

But growth is not always in adding.

Sometimes, it's in subtraction.

In simplifying.

In standing still and saying:

"I do not need to prove my worth through overextension."

"My peace is more valuable than your temporary approval."

"I am allowed to rest. To pause. To choose."

There is a sacred kind of power in knowing your enoughness.

You don't have to chase it in others' validation.

You don't have to purchase it through constant giving.

You don't have to earn it by being available for everyone all the time.

You are already enough – without the applause.

Saying No as Self-Trust

Saying no is not about being harsh.

It's about being **clear**.

It's trusting yourself to know when something doesn't feel right.

It's trusting your gut even when your mind tries to rationalize discomfort.

It's choosing your values over people-pleasing.

And it's holding space for guilt to rise – and still standing firm.

Because guilt isn't always a sign you're doing something wrong.

Sometimes, it's a sign you're doing something *different*.

Real-Life Reflection

You'll lose some people when you start saying no.

But you'll find yourself.

And you'll find the ones who never needed you to shrink in order to love you.

You'll disappoint some expectations.

But you'll stop disappointing your soul.

You'll disappoint a few plans.

But you'll start showing up fully in the ones that matter.

"Boundaries are not about keeping others out – but about keeping your inner world sacred."

You can still be kind – and say no.

You can still be generous – and set limits.

You can still love people – and not rescue them from their own consequences.

Because you are not responsible for carrying everything just because you're strong.

You're not obligated to keep showing up in spaces that take you for granted.

You're not required to keep saying yes to things that cost you sleep, sanity, or soul.

"Your no doesn't need explanation. Your boundary doesn't need a backstory. Your peace doesn't need permission."

The Note

"You do not owe your life to anyone's comfort.

You do not need to be liked to be worthy.

And you do not need to explain your boundaries to those who benefit from your lack of them."

Choose peace over performance.

Choose rest over rushing.

Choose yourself – softly, consistently, and without apology.

You just have to say:

"No, thank you. I choose myself now."

And that –

softly, clearly, sacredly –

is enough.

Chapter 10
The Love You Deserve Begins with You

"The relationship you build with yourself sets the tone for every other connection in your life."

We spend years chasing love in others.

Waiting for someone to see us, choose us, stay with us.

We long to be held in ways we've never been –

to feel safe, adored, valued, whole.

So we give.

We give everything.

Pieces of time.

Pieces of silence.

Pieces of our softness – even when it's unreturned.

We romanticize people who barely reach for us.

We turn crumbs into feasts.

We confuse temporary attention with lasting affection.

All because we are terrified of the silence that comes when no one is choosing us –

forgetting that *we can choose ourselves.*

Because the deepest kind of love – the kind that saves you, the kind that *stays* –

doesn't come from someone else.

It comes from you.

"Love that doesn't begin within will always come at the cost of your soul."

The Illusion *of love is loud. Real love is steady.*

When we think of love, we often imagine a perfect story.

We think love is someone texting us "good morning" every day.

Someone who never makes us cry.

Someone who always understands us – even when we say nothing.

Someone who stays close, no matter how messy life gets.

Someone who makes all the pain of the past disappear.

We believe love will feel like magic –

Fast replies. Long calls. Surprises. Promises. Fireworks.

We believe that love means **finally feeling complete**, as if another person will fix everything we feel is missing in us.

We grow up with these ideas from movies, TV shows, songs, and even people around us.

So we start expecting:

That love should always feel exciting

That our partner will always make us feel special

That if they truly love us, they'll never hurt us

That they'll always choose us, without question

But these are just dreams – **not reality**.

Because of these ideas, we:

Stay in relationships where we don't feel safe, just because it "used to feel like love"

Keep waiting for someone to change, thinking love will fix them

Blame ourselves when someone doesn't treat us well

Think we need to work harder to be loved

Confuse attention with love, and silence with distance

We forget that real love is not perfect.

It's not a fantasy.

It doesn't always look like what we imagined.

For a long time-

You mistook attention for care.

You thought silence meant patience.

You believed inconsistency was better than loneliness.

You held on to people who felt heavy, just to avoid feeling empty.

You gave love like it was air – essential, constant, unquestioned –

while hoping someone, someday, would finally love you back the same way.

But slowly, reality broke through the illusion.

They didn't show up.

Or they did – but not fully. Not safely. Not with the love you deserved.

And you began to understand:

You were never asking for too much.

You were just asking the wrong person.

That truth is painful. But it's also freeing.

Because once you stop trying to change others, you begin to change yourself.

You begin to see how often you've abandoned yourself for the comfort of others.

You notice how you softened your voice, held back your tears, or ignored your needs – just to avoid making someone else uncomfortable.

You realize that the version of you they couldn't love was the version you were never meant to edit in the first place.

And with that realization comes something gentle but powerful:

You don't have to chase love anymore.

You can create it – inside you.

Real love doesn't begin with someone holding you.

It begins when you learn to hold yourself – through the storm, through the silence, through the breaking.

When you sit with your own sadness without running from it.

When you forgive yourself for not knowing better.

When you stop waiting for someone else to come save you and instead whisper to your own heart: *"I've got you now."*

That is love.

That is safety.

That is home.

Yes, there's grief in this journey.

You grieve the fantasy of what you thought love would be.

You grieve the people who couldn't meet you where you were.

You grieve the years you spent thinking you had to be more, just to be worthy.

But beyond the grief, there is something else:

Hope.

Because now you see it clearly –

You were never broken.

You were never too much.

You were never unlovable.

You were simply asking people to give you something they didn't know how to give.

And now you are learning to give it to yourself – gently, daily, completely.

You were always enough.

Not when they noticed you.

Not when they chose you.

Not when they apologized.

Not when they stayed.

But before all of that.

From the very beginning.

So let them go. Let the old story fall away. Let the illusion die.

You don't need to be rescued.

You've already been found –

By you.

And in that discovery,

you rise.

When you begin to love yourself – really love yourself –

You stop waiting for others to see your worth.

You stop begging for attention from people who are too distracted.

You stop lowering your standards just to keep someone in your life.

You stop apologizing for your needs, your emotions, or your boundaries.

Instead, you start choosing:

Peace over chaos.

Truth over pretending.

Respect over attachment.

Growth over comfort.

You begin to **nurture your own heart** the way you once hoped someone else would.

You speak to yourself gently.

You listen when your body says, "*I'm tired.*"

You protect your energy from what drains you.

You stop blaming yourself for the ways others couldn't love you.

And something powerful happens.

When you deeply love yourself –

You stop **settling for half-love** and mixed signals.

You stop **begging for crumbs** of attention and affection.

You stop **believing that someone leaving means you're unlovable.**

You understand that someone walking away doesn't mean you're not enough –

it just means they weren't meant to stay.

You learn that **being alone isn't being unloved** – it's being with the one person who will never leave you: *you.*

You begin to enjoy your own company.

You make your own space feel safe.

You create a life that feels full – not because of who is in it,

but because of how deeply you've chosen to show up for yourself.

You realize

Your peace is not worth sacrificing for temporary attention.

Your heart doesn't need to be fixed – it needs to be held.

Your worth doesn't rise and fall with how others treat you.

And love isn't something you find – it's something you become.

Because once you become love,

you don't chase it anymore – you attract it.

And you never again forget this simple truth:

You can be your own home.

Warm. Steady. Whole.

YOU ARE NOT TOO MUCH.

YOU ARE NOT TOO LITTLE.

YOU ARE JUST RIGHT.

The Lesson

"The love you've been begging others to give you is the love you must first pour into your own heart."

You don't need a mirror to believe in your beauty.

You don't need a text to feel desired.

You don't need their presence to prove you're lovable.

You are love – in your breath, your scars, your softness, your truth.

You are worthy – even if they walked away.

You are enough – even if no one said it out loud.

So start now.

Romanticize your healing.

Spoil your solitude.

Protect your peace like a sacred vow.

And know this:

When you finally love yourself the way you once begged to be loved,

you will stop chasing people who only loved you halfway.

You will stop proving.

You will start *glowing.*

And everything –

everything you thought would come from someone else –

will begin blooming from within.

Chapter 11
Learning to Breathe Again

So, you forgot how to breathe?

Welcome to the club.

Not the medical kind. The emotional one.

You know – the one where you keep saying, *"I'm fine,"* with a smile so tight it could crack your jaw... while your soul quietly whispers, *"Actually, I'm drowning in three layers of unprocessed trauma, unmet expectations, and existential dread."*

Sure. You are fine.

We all are.

Let's Talk About This Magical "Breathing"

Apparently, breathing is natural.

Unless, of course, you have been busy **people pleasing, self-abandoning,** and **pretending you are chill** with every boundary being stepped on like a doormat on sale.

So yes, somewhere between *"Be strong"* and *"Don't be too much"*,

you stopped breathing – emotionally speaking.

You shrank.

You paused your needs.

You got really good at playing the version of yourself that everyone else felt comfortable around.

Congratulations. You became digestible.

And miserable.

The Turning Point (Cue Existential Crisis)

Then one day, you wake up.

Not with clarity – oh no – but with exhaustion so deep it makes even the thought of replying *"haha"* to a text feel like climbing Mount Everest.

And you think, *"Wow. Is this it? Is this what being alive means? Scrolling, surviving, suppressing?"*

And just like that, some voice inside you – probably your long-lost intuition – mutters:

"Girl, breathe. Not the shallow kind. The real kind."

Of course, that's hard. Because breathing means **feeling.**

And feeling means facing all the things you've expertly avoided with distraction, overthinking, or Netflix.

Healing doesn't come with a grand entrance.

It doesn't knock loudly or announce, *"You're okay now."*

Instead, it arrives like a sigh you didn't realize you were holding in for years.

A breath that flows in and out – quietly, gently – without the panic that once lived in your chest.

It begins when you notice the mornings don't sting as much.

When the ache doesn't greet you before your feet hit the floor.

When you stop bracing yourself for heartbreak that's no longer happening.

That's when it begins.

Not when the pain disappears...

but when *you* stop disappearing inside it.

"There is power in your quiet return."

You won't even realize it at first.

You'll simply move through a day without collapsing.

You'll laugh at something small – and mean it.

You'll stand in the sunlight, and instead of feeling exposed, you'll feel warmed.

You won't feel healed.

You'll just feel *present.*

And that will be enough.

Because for so long, your body only knew tension.

Your soul only knew survival.

Your heart only knew protection.

And now, something softer is returning –

not loudly,

not all at once,

but like light through a curtain: slow, gentle, steady.

You are learning to breathe again.

Not because the world is perfect.

Not because everything makes sense.

But because you've finally stopped abandoning yourself to make others comfortable.

You no longer need to be okay for anyone else.

You no longer need to fake resilience.

You no longer need to perform your healing to prove you're worthy of peace.

You've earned this softness.

You've walked through fire and didn't let it burn your soul.

Now you're learning to live without the armor.

And yes – that takes courage, too.

"Peace doesn't arrive as a reward. It returns when you stop running from yourself."

"Healing isn't loud or obvious. It's the moment you start choosing yourself in silence – and your breath doesn't shake when you do."

There will still be days when grief visits.

Still moments when old wounds knock on the door of your memory.

Still times when your heart feels tender, uncertain, exposed.

But you no longer run.

You sit with the ache.

You breathe through the discomfort.

You anchor yourself in presence, not perfection.

That's what healing is.

Not erasing the past – but learning how to live beside it without fear.

Not proving you're okay – but knowing you're safe, even when you're not.

So keep breathing.

Even when it's shaky.

Even when it hurts.

Even when no one sees how hard it is.

You're not just healing –

You're *becoming.*

And with every breath,

you're coming home to the version of you that always deserved to feel light again.

You Were Never Meant to Hold Your Breath Just to Be Loved

Somewhere along the way, many of us learned to **tighten ourselves** to fit into other people's comfort zones.

We called it love –

When we constantly said yes to avoid being left behind.

When we silenced our emotions to avoid being "too much."

When we shrank in conversations just to keep the peace.

But here's the truth:

If you have to abandon yourself to be accepted – you are not being loved, you are being tolerated.

Healing begins when we realize this.

When we stop adjusting ourselves like furniture in someone else's home.

When we stop holding our breath in relationships, workplaces, even in front of mirrors.

Learning to breathe again means:

Giving yourself permission to **feel fully**.

To say, "I don't like this," without guilt.

To exist loudly, honestly, and imperfectly – even if not everyone applauds.

Because you don't need a room that praises your silence.

You need a space that celebrates your presence.

And that space?

You create it – by choosing *you* over performance.

By remembering that the only love worth having is the one that lets you **breathe freely** – not carefully.

Chapter 12
Forgiveness Isn't About Them

"Carrying the weight of what someone did to you is like drinking poison and hoping they get sick."

Forgiveness is one of the most misunderstood forms of healing.

They say you *should* forgive.

They say it's the *right* thing.

They say *you'll feel lighter afterward.*

But no one tells you how complicated it feels.

No one tells you that forgiveness can look like rage, silence, grief, and distance – all at once.

No one talks about the ache of forgiving someone who never apologized.

Someone who moved on like your pain was a footnote in their story.

And so, for a long time, you hold on.

To the anger.

To the memory.

To the hurt – not because you want to stay wounded,

but because releasing it feels like letting them off too easy.

You carry it in your body.

In your jaw when it clenches.

In your chest when it tightens.

In your stomach when you hear their name.

It doesn't matter if it happened years ago –

trauma doesn't live in time.

It lives in the nervous system.

But let's be honest:

Some things aren't okay. Some wounds don't deserve excuses.

And not everyone earns a second chance.

And yet, there comes a moment –

a quiet, exhausted, sacred moment –

when you realize:

You can't keep bleeding for someone who stopped showing up long ago.

Resentment is a prison.

It doesn't trap the one who hurt you – it traps *you*.

It makes you relive the moment. Over and over again.

You replay the betrayal.

You rehearse the pain.

You build a fortress of anger just to feel safe.

But what if that fortress is also what's keeping joy out?

What if clinging to the grudge is what's keeping you stuck in the very chapter you're desperate to leave?

Forgiveness is not for the weak.

It's for the wounded who are ready to *heal.*

It's for the ones who are tired of dragging around bitterness like armour.

It's for the souls who want to be **free** – not just from the person, but from the story.

"To forgive is to set a prisoner free and discover that the prisoner was you."

– *Lewis B. Smedes*

So no – forgiveness isn't about them.

It doesn't require their apology.

It doesn't need their understanding.

It doesn't even ask for their presence.

Forgiveness is a decision you make quietly – for your own peace.

It's when you stop trying to rewrite the past and start reclaiming your future.

You get to say:

"Yes, that happened.

Yes, it hurt.

But it no longer owns me.

I am not the pain.

I am what survived it."

Forgiveness is how you close the door without slamming it.

It's how you walk away without burning the whole house down.

It's how you free yourself – not because they're worthy – but because *you* are.

"You don't forgive them for them. You forgive to free the version of you that's still stuck in the moment it all went wrong."

Forgiveness isn't a gift you give them.

It's a release you give to yourself.

It's choosing to stop rehearsing the betrayal in your mind.

To stop rewriting the conversation that never happened.

To stop looking for closure in a door they already locked.

It's not saying what they did was okay.

It's saying:

"I will not let what you did keep echoing through my life anymore."

You let go – not to forget,

but so you can remember yourself beyond what they broke.

You don't need to talk to them.

You don't need to sit in the same room.

You don't even need to understand why they did what they did.

You just need to decide that your peace is more valuable than your resentment.

Forgiveness doesn't erase the pain.

It doesn't rewrite what happened.

It doesn't mean what they did was right.

But it *does* mean that you're choosing **not to let it define you anymore.**

You are choosing **light over bitterness, peace over revenge,** and **freedom over resentment.**

You are not walking away as a victim –

You are walking forward as someone who has *reclaimed their power.*

So close this chapter with softness, not spite.

With strength, not shame.

With a heart that says:

"I did not forgive because they were sorry.

I forgave because I was ready to stop suffering."

"I forgave not to free them – but to finally free myself from carrying what was never mine to hold."

And that...

is how you begin again.

"The Unclenching"

I carried the wound
like it was mine to cradle,
like the pain was proof
I had once mattered
to someone
who let me shatter quietly.
I replayed the scene
until even my breath
felt like betrayal –
as if healing meant
they got away with it.
But then one day,
I grew tired
of bleeding in silence
for someone
who had long stopped
being haunted
by what they broke.
And so, I let go.
Not with a scream.
Not with fire.

But with a soft, trembling whisper:

"I forgive you — not for you,
but for the girl in me
who still flinches
when she remembers."
Now, I carry
not the wound,
but the wisdom.
Not the ache,
but the knowing:
I survived.
And I no longer need
your shadow
to feel whole.

Chapter 13
You Are Not Broken, You Are Becoming

You are not in pieces – you are in process.

"What if healing was never about fixing what's broken... but about remembering what was always whole beneath the hurt?"

There will be moments – quiet, aching moments –

when you sit with yourself

and wonder if you're still capable of softness.

If too much has been taken,

If too much has changed,

If maybe... you are beyond repair.

You'll touch the places that still feel tender.

The memories that still sting.

The parts of you that once lit up, but now only flicker.

And the lie will creep in again:

"I'm broken."

But hear this, deeply:

You are not broken.

You are becoming.

What cracked wasn't your spirit – it was the mask you wore to survive.

What collapsed wasn't your worth – it was the weight of what was never yours to carry.

You are not in ruins.

You are in rebirth.

"You are still whole, even if you had to rebuild yourself from the silence up."

This is what becoming looks like:

It's messy.

It's slow.

It's full of stops and starts.

It's days where you feel powerful and untouchable –

and nights where grief still knocks the wind out of you.

It's letting go of timelines,

letting yourself unfold,

letting your soul breathe – even if no one claps for it.

You're not behind.

You're not too much.

You're not incomplete.

You are simply **in the middle of a transformation no one can see but you.**

And that's sacred.

"There are no gold stars for pretending you're fine. There is only peace when you finally stop apologizing for how long healing takes."

You don't need to rush this.

You don't need to "go back" to who you were before everything fell apart.

You were doing your best

But you... you are building something wiser now.

A self who speaks with more truth.

Who moves with more care.

Who no longer shrinks just to fit into someone else's comfort.

You don't need to be perfect to be whole.

You don't need to be strong to be worthy.

You don't need to be healed to deserve love.

All you need to be – is **real.**

Affirmation

"You are not what happened to you.

You are what you chose to build with what remained."

You were never broken – just reshaped.

You bent under the weight, but you didn't shatter.

You paused, you questioned, you unraveled –

but you *kept going.*

Becoming is not clean.

It's messy, sacred, painful, and real.

And through every fall,

every silence,

every soft rebuild of self...

You were not falling apart –

you were falling *into* yourself.

Let go of the narrative that says you need fixing.

You are not ruins.

You are the raw material of something extraordinary.

This isn't the end.

This is the becoming.

And you are more whole than you've ever been.

A Letter to the One Who Stayed

"In the end, it wasn't them – it was you who stayed. And that made all the difference."

"You kept showing up – not because it was easy, but because something deep inside you refused to give up. That something is who you truly are."

This chapter is not written to the one who left.

Not to the one who hurt you, misunderstood you, or never showed up.

This is for the one who stayed.

Dear you,

I don't know how you did it.

I don't know how you kept going

on the days when everything inside you said, *"Just stop."*

I don't know how you kept giving

when your own hands felt empty.

How you kept loving

when you weren't being loved back.

I don't know how you carried so much,

spoke so little,

and still smiled

when no one saw the ache behind it.

But you did.

You stayed.

You stayed when people left.

You stayed when life got quiet.

You stayed even when you doubted if staying was worth it.

And I need you to know:

That wasn't weakness. That was sacred strength.

Final Lesson

No one saved you.

Not love. Not luck. Not time.

You saved yourself – piece by fragile piece, in the dark, when no one was watching.

That is not survival. That is power.

You didn't just stay –

you fought.

Every lonely night you didn't give up.

Every morning you rose, carrying a heaviness no one else could see.

Every breath you took, even when it trembled –

was an act of rebellion against the pain.

You weren't waiting to be rescued.

You were learning how to rescue yourself.

And you did.

Not loudly.

Not all at once.

But in the quiet, in the chaos, in the mess –

you built yourself from the wreckage.

And now, look at you.

Not broken.

Not begging.

Not empty.

But whole.

Holy.

Here.

You became the very thing you thought you were missing.

The very love, the very strength, the very shelter.

You became your own safe place.

So no – you are not just someone who made it.

You are someone who *remade* it all –

with bare hands, a wild heart, and the fire that never went out.

This is who you are now.

And nothing, no one, no past can take that away.

Dear you,

If you're reading this...

you made it.

Maybe not all healed.

Maybe still heavy in places.

Maybe still stitching yourself back together in silence.

But you made it.

You stayed.

And that means more than any polished ending ever could.

This book wasn't written to inspire.

It wasn't meant to wrap pain in pretty words.

It was meant to tell the truth –

the raw, unfiltered, trembling truth

of what it feels like to come undone...

and still choose to live.

I didn't write these chapters from a place of certainty.

I wrote them from the middle of my own ache.

From nights I wanted to disappear,

from mornings I didn't recognize myself in the mirror,

from the breathless moments I questioned if I'd ever feel whole again.

And I wrote them for you.

For the version of you

who's been holding everything together in the dark,

without applause,

without rescue,

without rest.

For the you who smiles in public but cries in silence.

For the you who keeps loving even when you feel empty.

For the you who's tired –

but still here.

Let this book remind you:

You are not weak for feeling deeply.

You are not broken for needing time.

You are not behind for healing slowly.

You are made of strength most people will never understand.

Because they didn't see the nights you didn't give up.

But *I do.*

And I need you to know –

you don't need to become someone else to be worthy.

You just need to come home to yourself.

Maybe life didn't go the way you planned.

Maybe love didn't look the way you hoped.

But you are still here.

Still becoming.

Still full of so much story left to live.

So if you forget everything else, remember this:

You stayed.

And that matters.

That *saves.*

Thank you for letting these words sit beside your truth.

Thank you for letting me hold space for your healing.

Thank you for surviving.

I see you.

With all the softness and fire in my heart.

Nisha Vishwakarma

Final Affirmation

For the one still becoming.

I am not here by accident.

I am here because I survived what tried to break me.

I don't need to be perfect to be powerful.

My wholeness was never lost – just buried beneath everything I was taught to silence.

Every scar on my heart is a map

of where I left pieces of myself and still chose to return.

I am not a story of pain –

I am the one who rose from it.

Even in the silence, I was growing.

Even in the darkness, I was becoming.

I do not chase validation anymore.

I validate my own softness, my own survival, my own strength.

I will never again apologize for how deeply I feel.

My emotions are not weakness – they are proof I'm still alive.

I honor the version of me who didn't give up.

I am here because they stayed.

There is nothing wrong with needing rest.

There is nothing wrong with still healing.

There is everything right

about choosing myself

again and again

even when it hurts.

I no longer shrink to be loved.

I rise in my truth,

and love finds me there.

Today, I do not pretend to be okay.

I *am* okay – because I finally let myself be real.

I am not broken.

I am not too late.

I am not alone.

I am becoming.

And that... is everything.

Thank You

Har Har Mahadev

Some griefs don't end.

They simply become a part of you – not as pain, but as wisdom.

And

One day, when you speak of them, you won't break – you'll bloom.

About the Author

Nisha Vishwakarma,

Writes straight from the heart. For her, writing is not just about words—it is about feelings that are too heavy to keep inside. Through her words, she tries to give voice to pain, silence, hope, and the quiet strength that lives in all of us.

She believes that even in the hardest moments, there is always a small light to hold on to. Her writing is a gentle reminder that broken things can still be beautiful, and every ending can carry the seed of a beginning.

Alongside her writing, Nisha works as a civil engineer in the public sector.

The Fire That Did Not Burn Me is her first book, born out of her own journey of falling, healing, and learning to rise again.

Instagram @_nisha_vishwakarma

https://www.nishaworld1998.wordpress.com

Thank you

for walking with me through these pages.
Every word I have written carries a piece of my heart, and if even a small part of it has touched yours, this journey has been worth it.

I am still learning, still healing, still finding my way—just like you.
And maybe that's the most beautiful thing: we are all works in progress, holding on to hope, one breath at a time.

With love,
Nisha Vishwakarma
(Civil Engineer by profession, writer by soul)